Her One Hundred and Seven Words

A prose poetry narrative

HER ONE HUNDRED AND SEVEN WORDS

A prose poetry narrative

Paul Hetherington

FARFLUNG EDITIONS
CHESHIRE, MASSACHUSETTS

FarFlung Editions
MadHat Press
PO Box 422, Cheshire, MA 01225

The Library of Congress has assigned
this edition a Control Number of
2021949601

ISBN 978-1-952335-36-5 (paperback)

Text by Paul Hetherington
Author photo by Fukahori Mizuho
Cover design by Phil Day
Cover image: *Knifed Bun* by Rachel Milne; oil on board

www.madhat-press.com

First Printing
Printed in the United States of America

For CA

Table of Contents

1. Clover

We tug four green leaves, chanting a rhyme you remember from school—only last year you were dressed in its uniform. Four stained tips of our interlocked fingers; four vows we make as we stand among green; months of knotted affection like this tussocky field.

2. Boston

You idealize the city of neighbourhoods, remember the haunt of your "now-dissolved" innocence. Your accent speaks of seven years there, when you walked every day in the Emerald Necklace and stood watching sky in Jamaica Pond, sailing a boat made from scraps of old ply. There were penned elephants at Franklin Park Zoo—the memory makes your hands shake with anger. I soothe your shivering arms.

3. Ballet

In the old concert hall boards creak and groan. Yet dancers in tutus astonish us both. We imagine ourselves in the lit world they conjure where birds and magic transform our poor knowledge. And perhaps we're gripped by dark enchantment and animal rhythms; perhaps we're lifted into realms of air where human feeling is clotted and cold. You lean on me dreamily, holding my arm, kissing me beakingly: "There's nothing can touch something so marvelous." I turn to see swans launch into air.

4. Dictionary

"I want to learn a new vocabulary." Day by day you make a list, exploring the dictionary, bringing examples into every room. "Caboose" and "clerestory" become the kitchen. You hand me "one hundred and seven words" in a miniature notebook—each one a gesture toward our living. A pocket-sized touchstone.

5. Poet

You say you're a poet but don't begin writing. It's a shapeless idea; a haunting of talk; an emblem of words in difficult spaces—as if between furniture; as if blowing and floating; as if wrenched from tongues and cast away.

6. Lipstick

Red denotes happiness—worn like a gash. Purple is an efflorescence, like a dark flower flagging "beware". Orange is trouble, as if the sun flames from your mouth with radiant discontent. Blue is an occasional choice, a symptom of joy or pain (finding out which is a minute's work). Pink elaborates childlike contentment—together, we smile at the world without prejudice.

7. Cherry

"It was raining," you said: "I sheltered beneath the tree but cherries stained my best white dress." Boughs twisted toward us, carrying our pasts. We were ghosts seeing words as crimson, rehearsing again a wish for coherence. The cherries are eaten; leaves won't protect us.

8. Lepidopterist

Three inner rooms of your father's house are filled with long cases of the beautiful creatures. Such a variety of lifting colors— the ghostly green of the Luna Moth; a Monarch displaying tiger stripes. A sense that time has alighted and been stilled by a pin. "They're like my lovers," you say—and I wonder whether I'll also be placed there, in the space of mind where feeling dies.

9. Triad

Two of us—together, apart, polarized, doubled in many convictions, yet always a third stands somewhere between us; as if we're looking over each other's shoulders at a further life implicit in our own. A third person speaks our words, occasionally our caresses feel another's hands. And in that summer, testing intimacy, both of us ask what could possibly constrain us: who is the person we fail to know?

10. Saffron

It tastes like a wide smile on your lips; yellows your fingers; gathers us into redolence, as if imparting a memory—brown shade and a leaning tree, your grandmother sifting threads and hours. It evokes the smell of something indefinable—wind, caress, childhood, the savor of an unexpected kiss, your grandmother's words: "marry well, be strict with yourself." We laugh, but you're momentarily sad: "What did I relinquish?" The bitter saffron tastes like tainted bliss.

11. Hotel

"In the middle of nowhere," you say when you book. And when we arrive after hours of driving, I'm inclined to believe you—the road's loose gravel and a surrounding golf course is lapped by swampland. The rooms are wall-papered in yellow and brown; the window looks over a wrecking yard. You shrug as a lorry trundles and squeals. You set up your easel, painting the sky. We stay for three days through banging and screeching as metal is rendered into reusable bits, and you ask to be held but cry when I touch you; we bury ourselves in depths of discomfort.

12. Mermaid

There are days when I imagine you as the ocean; months when you're a muscular mermaid; hours of swimming together in bed; a hundred weeks of breasting language. One day you're distant, diving and surfacing. Though I swim out I fail to find you in the jittery waves.

13. Clam

We might be infaunal, buried in conviction's sediment; burrowing, even as we seek each other, unaware how bivalve lives won't join. That February we're planted firmly, and no currents of language will shift what we know—you in your separateness, filtering cold currents; I in warm water, flushed by unknowing.

14. Nook

It is our place of forgetting all other places; a harbor and mouth. It's quiet evening at noon, words stilling, a way of travelling far within another's reach. A slow impress and solitude; the sense of a corner taken at speed.

15. Cats

You hold them like children, nursing, petting them. A lively wildness falls from their eyes. Their muscular climbing harvests birds; insouciant clawings unsettle the cherries. They jump at moths and snap at butterflies; sometimes beauty disappears in their mouths. In winter their coats thicken like luxury while we're plainly dressed in gathering feeling—the cats are outside a slammed-shut door.

16. Periwinkle

Through the wood—a mist, the uncurling of ferns, a meadow, an untrodden way. Periwinkles star the grass with blue and violet turnings, holding the sun in five-petalled grief. You laid the flowers on your mother's coffin; her absence turns through every day.

17. Keats

On your shelf a collected poems—"more happy, happy love!"
You say the phrase like a conviction, as if wanting to believe.
One night I read you the complete ode and afterwards you will
not speak. We sit in evening's brown fall with a sense of the
yellow leaf: your mother's death; our love's failure to thrive.
I think of unheard melodies and, beneath our apartment,
someone begins to play a flute. It might be from the Andes; it
might be piping against solitude.

Paul Hetherington

18. Oyster

What did you bring to the table that day? We ate three plates of estuary oysters, lifting each shell, placing them down. A clack on the plate, a burr on the tongue, plumping years corralling the mouth.

19. Lover

To be lovers doesn't close our thirty-five years. To be intimate isn't to be jointly spoken. To be separate is not to unfix mutuality. But if love is a church, its discordant bell pitches us apart. The ringing persists. Riddling agreement is our ground of dispute.

20. Penis

You collect small prints of males erect, and point to symbols in novels and plays—the leg in the boot, the spire, the oar. "They're all very 'Freudian,' as you would say, but it's the thing itself I most admire."

21. Glitter

You wear it on your face like speckles of undefined glory. It becomes you so well I'm soon entranced. Your eyes glitter too, as if brimming new tears. Which I guess they are, given your past—this signature of unhappiness.

22. Fingers

Old growths encrust the rocking jetty, like natural sculptures. Paintings fall from your gesturing fingers as if inscribed on the air. There's bright vermilion in your exclamation: "shapes of evening." We color meaning like mixing pigment; our palms are a pressure of unstated need. Water skips like a spirited child: "Can I have a baby with you?"

23. Sliver

A gasp of light. Where we lie, at the end of planning our holiday—hotels, restaurants and connecting trains. For dreamy minutes, in a sliver of sunshine. You say, "It feels so odd to be here." We dress in morning's equivocal knowledge, knowing little of what we have brought.

24. Scarlet

The color of saying what you hadn't intended. Our laughter, and silence; the kiss of evening against historic walls. My reassurance; your sense of exposure. "I've never said it to anyone else: my father's a bastard." Venice's canals are brown in the day's subsidence. Gondolas are docked. "There's no one in love"—except, despite anger, perhaps we are.

25. Stasis

Movement and stasis seem nearly identical. We won't move forward; we keep on traveling. We can't agree; we continue to try. We refuse to believe, denying our failure. Stasis and movement are much like each other. We find close sunlight in many rooms. We locate the same artists in various cities. Vermeer peers through four different portraits. But often we forget to know what we saw.

26. Opus

Our chief work is ourselves; our main writing occurs in air. A bookful; a wide margin of gesture. Your touch illuminates my skin as if it's vellum; we consume each other's words as if reading them by mouth—extravagances and excoriations alike; we are our own, naïve characters; makers of a plot without end. We think our book will remain open for many thousands of days.

27. Lark

We listen to the lark's elaborations singing outside a small window: "It's voice that matters most." You hold a high note, and your hands follow the song. It's as if the tune speaks for us from a distant century. This, in a week when affection is most of what we carry between us; when we practice our versions of the lark's thirteen elaborate voicings; when we touch each other's tongues as if finding the throat of love.

28. Unbound

"The freedom's marvelous." We stop at a bar. The old city's starlings swirl and carouse, as if dark emanations of irascible air; as if time warps and unwinds there. You sip and we gather our mutual months. "I'd like to paint the whole damn scene."

29. Angel

You're no angel, yet sometimes I feel a wide compassion wrapping you like wings. You stand in youthful separateness so often that you might be an unearthly visitor—strong, pushing back my affection. When you relent, still we have to find a way, as if bodily life has only just arrived. Your intricate tenderness is an excruciation.

30. Diaphanous

How aureate your skin looks in light; how your words sound as if they're light seen through fabric. In the small church you summon your mother's spirit, but it won't return. Whitewashed walls reflect candlelight; you hide your face with a scarf's thin silk, washed into grief. If you were cloth, you'd be diaphanous. The power of your sorrow stands me apart: "I cannot love you in this way."

31. Macabre

Arm in arm in London at night, and a young man falls in front of us. The blood on his shirt back is a wide, black rose—and, in better light, a petaled weal. You drop your handbag and cradle his head. He murmurs "I love you"—though you don't know his name—and a siren approaches like a stage-managed scream. As he's driven away the blood on your shirt curls.

32. Clandestine

In almost everything we do you insist on the clandestine. You disguise yourself at a market, hood pulled over your hair. I press feelings down, like something in a can. There are moments we risk a public embrace: in a coastal public garden; on a street in Japan. But nothing of us is written in the usual course. Sometimes a frisson, sometimes frustration, it inflects what we know. A kiss in a dark room. A performance with an audience of two.

33. Shakespeare

You say you've suffered a sea-change; that your father is dating a woman your age; that everything's untimely. I buy a margarita too encrusted with salt; I buy pearls you say are death's eyes. You claim your mother's ghost visits nightly and you lack decisiveness. We watch *As You Like It* and you begin to cry with a humorous sadness—"If only I was not who I am."

34. Moon

Symbol of subtlety, you adore its yellow light: "the seasons of women are made by the moon." Symbol of love, you doubt its power: "Love won't keep—the moon tells us that." We walk in a garden just after midnight and the moon turns toward us a face of grief. You recollect your mother's persistent travails: "to be so unhappy." The moon disappears as a rain squall gathers; I think of ancients who worshipped its face. I see myself standing on a bright wintry evening searching the moon for my own belief.

35. Gloaming

"What holds and belongs?" you ask as evening's luminous forgetting falls on the earth. You place your hand over my wintry heart: "Can it be true that we're here and in love?" I remember my vows to my former wife; how we both ignored what we seriously said. I remember my son who abandoned us both, saying he hated recrimination. "It's all the same," I find myself saying, not sure what I mean, suddenly angry. "It doesn't matter"—you're terse and wild—"your belief in me is surely enough."

36. Swain

"You're no youth but you may be my swain." You laugh and pull your dress up your legs. We try to fathom the Middle Ages in probing the meanings of that single word. "You might be a shepherd," you say as we try, "with my wool, your crook and this lanolin."

37. Ball Gown

Expensive and voluptuous, the gown becomes you, falling from your high waist toward the floor. I'm lost in the reds and purples, as strobes of remembering strike my coat—how once we said "maybe," drinking in a bar, and "surely we're perfect" as you swirled the gown. In that Spanish town we danced.

38. Soliloquy

So many soliloquies, we might be actors strutting the stage. So much to protest and enunciate—the world's lack of justice; the loss of species; a hundred mutual refusals. So much construction to dismantle murmur's edifice. So many words undoing kisses.

39. Cinnamon

Nearly the colour of your hair; not quite the scent on your skin; sometimes the taste on your tongue. A flavor never to be unpeeled from our mutuality. I think of you every time I place furls of bark in a pan. Each quill's a way of writing you into mind; each flight of fancy is a bird collecting aromatic sticks from the wide unknown. Our words weight their nests and the fragile sticks tumble. We pick up what's fallen, tying it with words. We gather fragrance as earnestly as thieves.

40. Whimsy

You leave me for an excruciating week, and on the fourth day I see you in a crowd, rounding a corner with another man. I think of a windlass collapsing; ore falling back into a gaping mine. Afterwards, you say it was an act of whimsy; a slate that expressed a revised sense of being—to find out how necessary I am: "Don't worry so much, it was a form of caprice." I believe it to be a strange subterfuge—a freakish extravagance.

41. Juniper

The name you most like—but not your own—according to some derived from Guinevere, the white enchantress. As a child you'd imagined yourself Lancelot's mistress beneath your backyard's juniper tree, marrying Mordred and later escaping from the awful convent (a twist in the story I enjoy). Sometimes you were Elijah hiding from Queen Jezebel, saying "And behold, the Lord passed by, and a great and strong wind tore the mountains."

42. Ineffable

What you don't state; the impossible ideas we entertain. A sense that we live in negative space and in speaking's shadow. Illogicality won't be admitted; ironies are rarely named. "We understand one another" encapsulates confusion. "We are happy" is a confession of discontent.

43. Sublime

"I fear for myself," you say decisively—"as if these vistas must overwhelm. They remind me of my father turning my corpuscles to riddles of stone. I imagined myself out-pinnacling mountains, yet here I am, as small as ever; as fleshly soft as anyone." We're in Switzerland above the clouds, having climbed for days through snow and rain. Our bodies are frail envelopes, holding squeezed identities. Three steps ahead are torrents of space.

44. Blush

The colour of words after you speak of your quandary. That first night together and its hue of new feeling. Evening's rumination on the river jetty. A Volstead crimsoning on the bar. The taint of our silence at 3 a.m. Your memory of something said in Boston. Our tincture of thought as we travel to Rome.

45. Blithe

On the Monday of our first anniversary blitheness falls like a carefree sense of who we are; and a dallying prospect of an impeccable future. You skip in the street, buying oysters for a vociferous beggar. Romans watch with mild interest, pushing strollers, hoisting shopping. We circle a pouting drinking fountain, filling bottles that overflow.

46. Sixteen

"Sweet sixteen": the phrase clots your speech. "When my father decided I was old enough." No second forgets your suffering; each clockface reminds you of lagging, supine minutes: "I try to bury it in the everyday." But meanings worm, as if from that yard with its toppling shed: "I'm lying there with bruised arms and mouth."

47. Griffin

You want a griffin to protect you from evil—"like the Persians,"
you say, "to tear out its heart." We sit by water but the waves
don't calm you—"so much injustice." You say your father
betrayed your belief; that the name of love is now turbid;
that he fractured beauty, promise and vow. It was much like a
painting in the palace of Knossos that someone retouched and
glued to a wall. The cracks remained beneath the pigment; that
glaring, horned creature once looked like a man.

48. Susurrant

The sound of memory bothers your sleep: ruminations on harm, like susurrant leaves. Sometimes you wander through the house for hours; sometimes you walk outside in rain. What we separately know sits stubbornly between us; what we brought to each other is strangely subdued. There's an undertone in all we say; meanings we make hear alternative murmurs.

49. Cuckold

Your father repeated it endlessly; how he'd been cuckolded; how you weren't his daughter. Yet, as a child, he forbade any test: "I don't need more proof. I know what I know." Later, after reports confirmed your relationship, you said "I'd prefer to be a bastard."

50. Vermilion

In Roman galleries the scarlet expanded—in the robes of citizens; on the bridles of horses. You thought of Mexico: "I want to be buried like the Mayan Red Queen." Your white teeth glinted as you remembered her mask—"such a serious look, such marvellous jade, and doused in vermilion like a wonderful bath."

51. Somnolence

You're often sleepy. We lie in bed with the ceiling fan clicking through noisy, wobbly rotations. Your dreams wake you in fits of cold sweat: "A monster; a bird I cannot describe." It plucks at your mouth with a long, hooked beak and tears at your legs: "I'm covered in blood." Sometimes I wake you and find you trapped in your father's soft words—like a shawl made of language cruelling your life.

52. Lolita

Being nineteen, you're no Lolita, yet you like the idea of being young—when you adored red roses and collected their petals; before they became an emblem of loss. Your thought is sometimes like high-flung clouds, your childhood strangely seen from above—a place pinked like fairy-floss when the world was new: the oldest color. You say, "I'm confused. Teach me to love."

53. Ellipsis

So much is ellipsis—what you think of your sister (you barely mention her); why your mother died ("I'll tell you later"); what your father's doing ("apart from his affair, no one would know"). We live in the gap between the before and after of all we discuss—our first tender words ... our subsequent chatter.

54. Requiem

You say that our care's a requiem—a way of remembering your mother's love. I scoff and you throw a book at me. "It's all I have—this act of redress." You mention an attempt at suicide and put a finger to my lips—"Don't ever talk of it. Don't lift the black hangman from his bottle." We drink red wine and toast the evening, listening to Mozart without repose.

55. Bed

We swim like dolphins in a hotel bed, huddle and grasp in a cheap bed-and-breakfast, straighten ourselves in a small single room. You say how you like it—to be forced so close. I say I enjoy an excess of space. We're always like that—asserting difference; pushing and pulling. You roll in a doona and ask me to find you. Then you're crying "about so many things." You lie like a doll in the Great Bed of Ware.

56. Crackerjack

In the boutique you say the word like an explosion, laughing at the price of the costly, sheer fabric. Dressed in it, you're an old-world vision, when nymphs climbed from rivers, or kings supped with courtesans: "Am I beautiful?" The large world tips toward your allure, like a vision from Ovid.

57. Esculent

Pale-skinned, with eyes the colour of aubergine, you say "I've been reading the dictionary. Now taste me like an apple or sweet dessert." In morning's light your skin shines like pastry and your blouse is a splash of grassy wine. You ask, "Am I esculent?"

58. Curmudgeon

Your name for me when I want to think and you want to talk, when I'm cross, or when we argue too much. Your frown says it all, signing the word before you speak, the crease in your lip announcing its coming. You emphasise the first syllable, as if to say, "you have nowhere to turn."

59. Opera

You sing your discord unforgettably—"I am leaving, this is intolerable, I don't know myself." The recitative resolves nothing but your voice continues to shrill through cold air: "I don't exist; you construe and constrain." Later, we walk by the river, looking for solitude. Birds fleck the air like black notes; everything adheres to that ruminating score.

60. Frore

We talk of language, wrapped in coats and scarves. Night is dark liquid in a sky-rimmed glass. So many words that the world's letting go: eftsoons, soothfast, wanion, endlong, hight. And the past participle, frore, meaning this unyielding, frosty night.

61. Popinjay

You call me conceited; upstart, full of self-regard. There's some truth in it, too. You say I had no right to be pleased with myself—"retired public servants are as common as soap." I try to protest but you wave my words away. My affection wavers and we stand apart. You kiss and name me "a member of the self-elect" and "my sweet, intolerable popinjay."

62. Wuthering

We were wuthering on a nearly still day. In thought, in conversation, wind-blown with pain. Your sister had emailed to say she disowned you. Your father had rung and promised a visit. You start to blame me for being "so old—no one approves." I feel wind in my mind. "I'm not your father" is what I say.

63. Starboard

The small yacht gallops and twists. "I feel sick," you exclaim, "let's go back to shore." A few minutes later you're "infinitely better," idling with your notebook, trying words, asking which side is starboard. I mention Old English and then quote Melville: "the directions he had given us about keeping a yellow warehouse on our starboard hand." "What the hell are you doing, spouting rubbish like that?"

64. Rome

Dark skies, graceful parabolas of starlings, a vast murmuration of birds. They need no instructions to make an airy ballet, while we fail to coordinate our choice of drinks. A Bloody Mary swirls in your hand. You say, "This city's beautiful but dirty. The galleries are wonderful but there's so many paintings. How many more can you possibly see?" I say it smells of many millennia; that I want to visit a gallery tomorrow. "A way," you ask, "of avoiding me?"

65. Postcard

A postcard arrives that makes you blush. You almost cry out, pursing sound within your mouth. I glimpse a blue scrawl. You hide it from view, deep in your handbag. "Is everything fine?" "Of course, we're here in this wonderful city ... It's from an old friend, it's nothing at all." "Are you sure you're happy?" "Yes— except for your silly questions." "What does your friend say?" "I'm not telling you."

66. Bubble

Rome is a bubble full of art and cafés. I speak of staying for another year. You prospect the idea of traveling back home. My feelings judder at the thought of relinquishment. You say, "It's impossible, I'm sticking with you." You hold me tightly against the wall and breathe in my ear. There are many small things—your post-coital sadness; your phrase for our apartment—"this house of blue light"—and the wine bars we love. You bite a fingernail and say, "Maybe not."

67. Legerdemain

We buy juggling balls in Rome's street market and, in the apartment, you throw four in the air. A blurring display, they hoop and dive like the starlings we'd watched, your hands becoming a conductor of flight; a definition of "legerdemain." Wide light strikes you from an open window; you stand apart in brilliance and skill. Later you say, "It kept me sane, standing in rhythm through four years of practice."

68. Rubicund

The face in the mirror, can that be me? The flush of your words; knife-twists of feeling; a sense that our love has reached a conclusion. Recomposing myself, marshalling anguish, telling myself I can manage the parting. Rubicund thought; rubicund memory. You turn and exclaim, "Ignore what I said. It's all okay."

69. Wherefore

Not "where" but "why." You enjoy the distinction. Yet our own whys and wherefores are never settled. "Because we love words; because we love touch; because you and I are both strangely lost." You give twenty reasons but none of them sticks. Or, all of them stick but none is enough.

70. Minotaur

"You are the minotaur and I'm Ariadne. If you catch me, I'm your sacrifice." I chase you around the small apartment and nearly trap you against the settee. But you're quick on your feet and duck past my hands. Then you ask for forgiveness from "the old, blood-soaked monster." You point to a ball of crimson wool. "Of course," I say. We pour red wine and you stroke my head: "I'm sure I saw horns as you charged at me."

71. Labyrinth

Sometimes our love is a Greek labyrinth. "I don't like your words. You're much too abstract." Or, "I prefer it when you're less precise." Or, "Why don't you cook a dinner for me? Wait, don't slice onions—I'd like to go out." You speak of your mind as a strange ferment—something that you'll never map ("There's no way out and no way through"). We walk the streets of south-eastern Rome, holding hands above ancient tunnels—a forgotten world below what we know.

72. Elixir

Your mouth is youth's elixir, and I taste it often. But one day you say, "Don't kiss any more." You stand on tiptoes to look from the balcony toward St Peter's and the Vatican City. "At seven I wanted to be a nun, serving God, asking for nothing. But a boy kissed my mouth and I got the taste of it. Sometimes I think of that young idea—a religious ecstasy of the spirit." We pour Tempranillo into thick, wide glasses, tasting wine that might have been blood. You kiss me again and smile as you do: "Sometimes this is almost enough."

73. Gossamer

We see it in autumn silvering the fields. You say, "It's like semen spread across grass." My tenderness toward you gathers my arms. You're suddenly the daughter I never had—an impossible feeling.

74. Tippet

Your long scarf falls down the front of your dress. "A tippet," I say, "like medieval garb." You wrap it to frame your lovely face, hold it as belt to cinch in your waist. You throw it around me, and draw me in. "How," you ask, "would we love without clothes?"

75. Tulle

Dressed in nothing but a kind of tulle. Beauty itself, with a shadowed allure.

76. Tutu

"From four to fifteen I went to ballet, learning all those difficult steps." You say you liked the daily rigor; that it took you away from school and sadness. Like a stream in the mind, you found your own flow in the pirouette and arabesque. "I loved the tutu; the pink gatherings of tulle; the way it transformed me from schoolgirl to dancer. I suppose I was stage-struck, but an injured knee put an end to those plans. And that's when my painting really got going." You stand on one leg and slowly turn in graceful repose. A swan on a lake or a feisty young woman—I wasn't sure which most suited your ardor.

77. Ingénue

"Am I the innocent in your worn life; the girl you seduced and will soon throw away? Or a character in some novel you're making, a woman you'll toy with and love just a little, but who you'll replace at the end of the year?" My protests fall around your cocked head; you drink half a bottle of very fine wine: "Hurry up, please take me to bed."

78. Affair

You say casually, "I like our affair." I say it's rare. You insist it's ordinary but has its moments. I compare it to an astonishing jewel. You say it will do for a few more months (and nod and frown). I say I adore you.

79. Insouciance

Your default position becomes a studied insouciance. "Perhaps I care" or "I'll care if I must." You speak of how your mother cherished you, bathing you in olive oil. "I might be piquant because of that practice." It's a sort of joke and you venture a smile. "She ran out of the house to escape my father and was hit by a car. I couldn't revive her." Evening is falling. "I'd love you better if I only knew how."

80. Lilt

Always a lilt in your voice, like a swaying curtsy of sound. Especially when reading books aloud—as if the words are choreographed. I listen to your rendition of *Middlemarch*, imagine you Dorothea, imagine I'm other than Casaubon. Your voice seduces me newly every hour.

81. Synecdoche

In our parts—legs, ankles, thighs, mouth—so we find the whole sensation. In our wholes—identities, names, our willing bodies—so we make love, searching our parts. Your lips kiss and speak of disaffection. My words mouth and fall into sensual disrepair. Hands follow contours of each other. Parts and whole are equally everywhere.

82. Bibliophile

I speak often of books, my true-hearted companions. You say I like words more than anything else, sometimes insisting: "read my body instead." One night we kiss on an uncomfortable sofa and you hand me Chaucer: "Speak it aloud." *The Knight's Tale* sounds the strangest of worlds, while you snuggle closely: "Read it again." Caressed by language we smell the old pages, content in their rapid iambic flow. You say we have tasted Chaucer's long tongue.

83. Conniption

"You forgot our anniversary—I guess you don't mind." I say I never think of such things. "If we were married our lives would be different." You leave the apartment for nearly an hour. When you return you hand me a simple ring: "A keepsake to remember me by." We kiss in the twilight as the gold on my finger blinks with my failings.

84. Fipple

As air through a recorder's fipple follows the ducted flue past the labium lip, so we make our own harmonious music.

85. Hands

Small and precise, with long fingernails, possessing gestures like storehouses of signs, clenched on some nights during furious sleep, artful in drawing a splinter away, deft in their watercolorist's touch, and always inflecting your soft, whirlwind speech.

86. Lullaby

Your improvised song's a lullaby, letting me sleep, washing my headache. You stroke my forehead, singing a story of how as a child in Boston you visited your aunt. She hoarded old newspapers in a shed in the yard and her fluting voice talked of husbands who'd died. "It was a strange Gothic scene. She walked around in curlers and nightie, dead-heading roses and making weak tea. My father's sister was stranger than he was."

87. Flood

Not of tears but of feeling, when I find you on the floor. You're pale and cold; I wrap a thin blanket. Minutes wind slowly with the anticipation of a siren. Eventually paramedics bundle you up. Your breathing's as shallow as an infant's in a cot; I bend to hear it.

88. Lagoon

Sleep catches me, drowning consciousness in the hot midday. I'm swimming in a wide lagoon and babbling about the nature of love. You're on the shore staring toward a figure in the hinterland. He lays out a picnic in the shade of a tree and beckons you over as I try to swim back to the pebbly beach. When I arrive, the picnic setting is covered in weeds. I begin to dig down, looking for remnants. Under earth your face is smiling, like a lively corpse. You speak suddenly and begin to stand up. In your hand is a scintillant knife.

89. Strings

The violinist leads the *Four Seasons* with bravura and a nearly impeccable intonation. I whisper to you about the poems inscribed in the score, and Vivaldi's instructions for "Summer": "Languor caused by the heat." It's August in Rome and after the concert we lie languorously with the tune in our ears near a wide-open window. You ask how something so old can move you so deeply; something so refined make you feel naked. "It's the effect of beauty," I say ineptly.

90. Crush

First me, that full feeling; then you felt it too—when everything between us was about to be made. For three complete months, our crush on each other. Lying in bed, I recollect it.

91. Unrequited

If it was "love," it had been requited. We'd both say so, despite our differences. Later you question the "prickly" word—"we are friends, first of all." In months that follow you claim we're companionable.

92. Film

The film *Kaos* stays with us, as if the raven's bell rings in the sky outside our apartment. You say, "That jar surrounds me every day, stifling breath—yet I too would slide down Lipari's pumice."

93. Cello

The sound of the Elgar concerto is slightly burnt caramel. Listening's a rapture like a child sucking sweetness again and again. "How was that imagined?" you ask, sitting for ten minutes after the concert hall empties, still hearing reverberant strings.

94. Afternoon

We loll, with the sound of a football game from the nearby park. You're distracted, suggesting we go for coffee, then changing your mind. I read *Tess of the d'Urbervilles*—appalled, as I'd been when nineteen, railing against the world. You try to read it and dislike the opening paragraphs. "Go on," I say. So you do, for three days, and on the last afternoon you place the novel in front of me. "Are we like that?"

95. Lollapalooza

You bear the large lollipop through the back streets of Rome, gleaming with reds and rainbows, like a torch to light the city. You suck on it casually, as if it means almost nothing, yet carry it for hours, inspecting shops, asking me to keep it safe, like contraband. Eventually it's half its size and you throw it away. Rain begins and we eat pasta at a café as starlings wheel overhead. You say I have changed.

96. Wolf

Seeker of trails, traverser of wilderness growing into unbiddable wild beauty. You gesture at a picture of the gray wolf, your hands curl, your nails are red. A dark mane of hair falls across your arched back. You're focused and intent, staring and alert, scenting your world.

97. Nympholepsy

I make my own Vari Cave near an imagined Attica. I don't dedicate it to Pan or Apollo but worship you through hundreds of cooked meals. I'm Archedemos in thrall.

98. Interlude

We oscillate between arguments and blitheness, as if we're by-products of that to-and-fro. A space that moves like tides: mostly interlude and never a pause.

99. Riven

Even in our fondest accord, lying in sunshine, holding each other like intertwined plants—the feeling in our bodies a slow blossoming—still we cross a divide. Our entanglements beleaguer us even while locating us; pleasure's aftermath leaves us like extended hands, uncertain what they reach for. Our suture pulls and pulls.

100. Dessert

Eating your fifth tiramisu that fortnight, you say this is the best of them, balancing sweetness and bitterness—succulent, firm, melting, inimitable. Our conversation about the future wanes; the dessert wine is yellow autumn in our glasses. We know so many layers of consideration yet I'm unable to name them—their archaeology's too complex. "This is superb," you say, digging with your spoon, glancing away toward the Roman night.

101. Thinking

We do it better than most—considering our options; querying the future. Our thoughts are like servants running in and out with the mail, or like lawyers debating in court. Many high ideas waft and settle, then are lifted again, as if contemplation is wind. When one of us tries to rest, the other opens a shutter overlooking a new vista; or is abstracted, trying to fathom what they see. We know our feelings in the same way, cross-questioning love.

102. Bliss

We know it for days. Holding, talking, being in each other's gaze, newly exposed, believing another's hand is everything of touch. It can never be spoilt. It has never been quite like this: bliss sliding on the body, like oil. Yet it carries an absurdity— the portended loss it won't recognize. Now it's a residue or smear. Its aftermath is its contradiction.

103. Cicisbeo

"I married at eighteen and have decided to go back." Rome's church bells explode in a shrapnel of sound. "Sorry I never told you." I walk the city even as I sit cradling an espresso. Buildings are black and white, as in a 1950s movie. I had a bit part, in the corner of a few scenes; a character later edited out. I ask you to say it again, although your enunciation was perfect. It's your final word: "I still love that man."

104. Sequin

I find it after you've left, caught between boards. Shining, it reminds me how we caroused, your ball dress swirling like the width of night. I throw it toward the gaping bin. So much heft and heaviness in such a trivial thing, and still it falls short. The first time it fell you were pulling at your blouse as I pulled at your skirt—such dramas of misjudgment.

105. Redolent

Of cheese we ate in London; of your scent, *Danger*, which may have been a warning—just faintly, like something unexpected in memory—of an unidentifiable sweetness, as if caramel was dropped there, and yet darker than that. Once I wore your scarf and it clashed with my jacket. A woman glanced a question; I put it away. I cannot give it back and will not wear it.

106. Belletrist

Fine words, fine letters. You inscribed a book with my name, your handwriting impeccable. It's an old French novel in translation; an idealisation of love. The characters speak of dreams among refined interiors. At the time I looked at the dingy café and knew it wouldn't translate. I wanted to justify myself. But the novel reminded me that there were so many different ways of speaking; that mine lacked elegance.

107. Saul

I think of falling out of a life; of Caravaggio's rendering of blinded Saul as he's reborn into a new name. I wonder if I could ever do it, sitting in St Peter's, hearing the Pope telling graduating students about the war for hearts and minds. His archaic words reverberate clearly around the heavy stone walls, as if seeking ascendancy. I cannot believe, wanting you to appear like a sudden angel and turn toward me with a wafer in your hand. Body and blood; it is sacrilege.

Acknowledgements

I owe a special debt of gratitude to Cassandra Atherton whose creativity, advice and editorial nous were crucial to the writing of these prose poems. I would also like to thank Michelle Hetherington and my daughters, Suzannah and Rebecca, for everything they contributed. And I owe a great deal to Marc Vincenz and the team at MadHat Press for their wonderful support and expertise.

About the Author

PAUL HETHERINGTON is a distinguished Australian poet. He has previously published 15 full-length collections of poetry and prose poetry, including the co-authored epistolary prose poetry sequence, *Fugitive Letters* (2020), and *Typewriter and Manuscript* (Life Before Man, 2020), along with a verse novel and 11 poetry chapbooks. He has won or been nominated for more than 30 national and international awards and competitions, most recently winning the 2021 Bruce Dawe National Poetry Prize. In 2014 he won the Western Australian Premier's Book Awards for the best poetry book published in Australia and in 2017 he was shortlisted for the prestigious Kenneth Slessor Prize. He undertook a six-month Australia Council Residency at the BR Whiting Studio in Rome in 2015–16. Paul is Professor of Writing in the Faculty of Arts and Design at the University of Canberra, head of the International Poetry Studies Institute (IPSI), and joint founding editor of the international online journal *Axon: Creative Explorations*. He founded the International Prose Poetry Group in 2014. With Cassandra Atherton, he is co-author of *Prose Poetry: An Introduction* (Princeton University Press, 2020) and co-editor of *Anthology of Australian Prose Poetry* (Melbourne University Press, 2020).

66580144R00078